ASHLEY

and

THE SOAPY SUDS

FLYING CLUB

Best Wishes!
Joe Blakey

ASHLEY

AND

THE SOAPY SUDS FLYING CLUB

by

J. BLAKEY

TANDEM HOUSE
Ontario, Canada

Thanks to Miss J. Alexander and the students of her Grade 3 class at Oakley Park Public School, Barrie, Ontario, who read this story and suggested improvements.
Thanks also to Ashley, Brittany, Kristine, Michael, Robert and Stephanie --- the greatest kids in the world!

Published by Tandem House,
A Division of 1084455 Ontario Inc
Kingscroft R. R. 1
Thornton, Ontario, L0L 2N0

Canadian Cataloguing in Publication Data

Blakey, Joseph
Ashley and the soapy suds flying club
ISBN 0-9680528-0-0
I. Title
PS8553.L35A85 1996 jC813'.54 C96-930963-5
PZ 7. B53As 1996

Printed and Bound in Canada

Chapter One

Ashley was sitting in the kitchen with her mom and her baby sister, Brittany. She was feeding Brittany a bottle of baby formula.

"I'm glad I've got a sister," Ashley said.

"Are you, sweetheart?" Mrs. Miller replied. When she was thinking about something, she didn't pay attention to what people said. This was one of those times. She was thinking of ways to keep Ashley occupied. It was the summer holidays. She didn't want Ashley to get bored.

She wondered if they should take a trip to Hart Lake. Ashley could invite her two best friends, Stephanie and Kristine.

"Brittany is so cute," Ashley continued. "I think the best time is when she wakes up in the morning. She doesn't cry. She just laughs and gurgles. And she moves her legs and arms real fast. Sometimes I think she's going to jump right out of her crib!" She laughed at that.

"Oh, I don't think she can do that yet," her mother said. "She's only five months old, you know." She still wasn't paying attention. She changed the subject suddenly. "Ashley, I've just thought of something. Let's go to Hart Lake this afternoon. It's a beautiful day. You can invite Stephanie and Kristine to come with us. What do you think?"

"That's a cool idea, Mom," Ashley replied. "I'll finish feeding Brittany, then I'll call on them. I'm sure they'll want to come."

She gave her sister the rest of the bottle and went to call on her friends.

Kristine was lots of fun. When everybody else was sad, Kristine could cheer them up with a smile and a joke. "Why did Grandpa give up tap-dancing?" she would ask. Everybody would groan and say, "Because he kept falling in the sink!" They knew all of her jokes. Most of them were corny.

Kristine could be serious about some things. She got really annoyed with people who spelled her name with a "C", instead of a "K". "I wish people would learn to spell," she would say crossly. "It should be easy to spell someone's name properly!"

Stephanie was quite different. She was tall, and she had long, blonde hair. She was quiet and serious. She would often ask difficult questions, like: "What are YOU doing to fight pollution?" Nobody had good answers to her questions.

Ashley didn't have far to go. She lived in a village

called Rosemount, and the village wasn't big. Stephanie and Kristine lived near one another, close to Memorial Park.

Kristine's house came first. Ashley went to the side door and knocked. Mrs. Kelly answered. She was dressed in a beautiful summer dress. Mrs. Kelly never wore jeans or shorts. She always wore a dress. It was always a pretty dress.

"Hi, Mrs. Kelly. I came to talk to Kristine. Actually, I should talk to you first."

"Come on in," Mrs. Kelly said. "Come to the kitchen and I'll get you a cool drink."

She called upstairs to Kristine, then she led Ashley into the kitchen .

"Make yourself comfortable," she said. "Kristine will be down in a minute."

She gave Ashley a glass of red pop, with an ice cube in it. It was Ashley's favourite soft drink.

"My mom's taking my sister and me to Hart Lake this afternoon," Ashley explained. "We wondered if you would let Kristine come with us. We'd be back in time for supper."

"Oh, can I go, Mom? Can I go ... PLEASE!" It was Kristine talking. She had heard the conversation as she walked into the kitchen. "I'd love to go with you, Ashley. Mom, please, can I go? Please, Mom, can I?"

Kristine wasn't a calm person. She'd almost had a heart attack when Brad Smith had bumped into her at school and sent her homework flying. Right now, she was very excited, though she probably wasn't going to have a heart attack.

"Calm down, Kristine," her mother said. "You'll make yourself ill if you go on like that. You've forgotten, haven't you? To-day's the day we have to go into town. You have to buy a dress to wear at your cousin Lisa's wedding. The wedding is only two weeks away. We have to get the dress now. I'm sorry, Ashley," she continued, "Kristine can't go to Hart Lake to-day. Perhaps to-morrow, but not to-day."

"That's okay," Ashley said as she left. "There'll be lots of other days, you know. This was kind of a last minute idea anyway."

She made her way to Stephanie's house. Her friend was sitting at the patio table writing. She was always writing. When she grew up, she was going to be a famous writer. So now she practised every day.

"What are you writing, Steff? Can I read it?" Ashley asked.

"You should read it," Stephanie replied. "It's all about endangered species. Did you know that right now there are over seven hundred endangered species? Seven hundred! " She paused, then added: "By the way, please don't call me Steff. I don't like it!"

Ashley didn't really want to discuss endangered species. She wanted to organise a trip to the beach. And she certainly didn't want to annoy her friend.

“Stephanie,” she said, “my mom’s taking me to the beach this afternoon. She wondered if you’d like to go with us.”

“Oh, no! I can’t,” Stephanie groaned. “This afternoon we’re visiting my aunt and uncle. They've just had a new baby. My mom and dad and Tim and me ... we’ll be gone for the rest of the day.”

Ashley was really disappointed. There was nobody else to ask. Stephanie and Kristine were her best friends. She didn’t feel like going to Hart Lake without them.

“If you don’t mind, Mom,” she said when she got home, “I think I’d rather just hang out around here. We can go to the beach one day next week.”

“As long as you’re sure you won’t be bored,” her mother replied.

“I’ll be fine, Mom,” Ashley said cheerfully. She wasn’t feeling so cheerful, but she didn’t want her mom to worry. “I’ll just go out into the garden for a while.”

Ashley enjoyed the summertime. There was lots to do. She could ride her bicycle or go for a walk. She usually did lots of things with Kristine and Stephanie, of course. They had picnics. Sometimes they went raspberry picking. Sometimes their parents would take them swimming in Hart Lake.

There was one thing that Ashley did a lot. She loved to make up stories. In the wintertime, she wrote stories on her dad's computer. In the summertime, she would often sit on the grass in the garden, blowing soap bubbles ...... and making up stories in her head!

One day she thought up a great story about being a famous ballet dancer. In her story, she danced on a huge stage, with hundreds of people cheering her. Afterwards, they threw flowers onto the stage. How exciting it was! Of course, she knew that it was just a story. She couldn't do ballet. There wasn't even a ballet teacher in the village.

Another day she made up a story in which she was a beautiful princess. In the story, she married a handsome prince. That story was quite nice, but it WAS a little boring, in her opinion. Princesses were pretty, but they didn't seem to do very much! When she grew up, she wanted a more interesting life than that. She would be a doctor, or maybe an airline pilot.

Ashley wanted one thing most of all. She wanted to travel. She wanted to see lots of places. In fact, she wanted to see the whole world!

She loved making up stories and blowing soap bubbles. She was an expert with soap bubbles. She started bubble-blowing with a kit she bought at the village store. There were only three things in the kit. There was a plastic ring with a handle on it. There was a little pouch of soapy liquid to make the bubbles, and there was a plastic cup to hold the liquid. The kit was okay, but it didn't make big bubbles that lasted a long time. So she experimented with other stuff, until she had her very own special liquid for blowing bubbles. She didn't tell anyone else what it was. It was her secret. That was why her bubbles were different from anybody else's. They were bigger. They lasted longer. And they had more colours.

That's what she would do this afternoon, she decided. She would sit in the garden and blow bubbles. Some people would think it wasn't a very exciting thing to do. But she knew better.

It turned out to be a lot more exciting than she imagined!

Chapter Two

Ashley was alone in the garden. Brittany was in her crib. Her mother had gone into town to meet a friend. Her father was in the house, babysitting.

She was blowing bubbles. Everything had to be just right. The right mixture. Of course, the right weather, too! The sun was really bright, and there wasn't much wind. That's why the bubbles seemed to be especially great today.

Ashley swirled the plastic ring in the secret formula, held it in the air and blew. She was so good at it that she could blow dozens of bubbles in just a few minutes. They shone in the sunlight. They were all the colours of the rainbow. She watched them drift up towards the blue sky. Some were tiny and burst quickly. Some were as large as tennis balls. They floated so beautifully. She envied them. They could float high in the sky, far above the grass and the trees. If she could float like that, she would be able to travel far away.

Then Ashley noticed something strange. There were

dozens of bubbles in the air, but one bubble was different from all of the others. It had the same bright colours, but it did not float away. It stayed on the ground! It was very close beside her. "What a strange bubble," Ashley said to herself. "Why doesn't it float away, like all of the others?"

Then she noticed something even stranger. The bubble was growing! It was getting bigger and bigger. Soon it was much bigger than a teacup. Very soon, it was bigger than Ashley herself! How surprised she was! She was also a little afraid.

She stared at the bubble. "How can this be?" she asked herself. "It has never happened before." That was true. She had never blown a bubble so big, or so beautiful, or so strong. It was magic!

She walked slowly around the bubble, looking at it very carefully. It was shiny and colourful. The walls were shaking a little in the breeze, but they seemed to be strong. There was nothing inside it. "So it's not a space ship from Mars!" she laughed to herself.

Then she had an idea. This bubble was big enough to live in! It wasn't as big as her bedroom, but there was lots of space to stand up in it. Could she get inside it? she asked herself. Of course ...... that was it! If she could get inside and make it move, she could travel! What a brilliant idea!

She looked towards the house. There was no one at the windows. Her father must be busy looking after

Brittany. There was no one on the gravel road that ran by the garden. She was all alone. Good. She would carry out her plan secretly.

She walked up to the strange bubble. The colours were very bright. The outside was shiny, like a mirror. It looked very strong. Is it really strong, she wondered. It seemed to have stopped growing, thank goodness.

Ashley walked right up to the bubble and placed both her hands on the sides. She pushed gently. Her hands sank into the bubble ... and there she was! Her hands were inside the bubble, and the rest of her body was outside. Very slowly, she moved her right foot towards the bubble and pushed. Now she had both hands and one leg inside! She moved the rest of her body to the bubble and slowly squeezed herself inside.

What a strange feeling that was! It felt a bit like swimming. She had done that at the lake. In a way, the water felt solid. It held you up and helped you to float. But it also made room for you. It didn't stop you moving around. Squeezing into the bubble was a bit like that, she decided. It felt good anyway.

It was a lovely bubble from the outside. It was even more beautiful from the inside. Ashley looked out and clapped her hands with joy. It was just as though she was in a house made of windows ... except that it was better, of course. Everything outside seemed to be covered with a beautiful mist of many colours. The houses, the garden, the trees, the grass, - everything was even more beautiful from inside the bubble.

"Now, what?" Ashley asked herself. "Here I am. I'm in the bubble, and the bubble has not burst. It seems like a very special bubble to me. What shall I do? Shall I get out of here and go back home? Or shall I do something really daring?" She frowned, wondering how she was going to decide. "I wish Stephanie were here, or Kristine," she said to herself. "I really need them right now. They would be able to help me to make up my mind. I can't stay here much longer, or someone will see me."

What a hard choice to make.

"I will not waste any time," Ashley decided. "I've waited long enough for this moment ... I'm going to go on a journey."

But how could she do that? The bubble was standing still. The answer came to her very quickly. She drew in a deep breath, deeper than any breath she had ever known. She held it until she was red in the face, and then she let it out slowly and gently. It worked! The bubble hesitated a little at first, then shook a little bit - and it began to move!

It rose very slowly in the beginning. First it climbed until it was as high as the cherry tree. Then it rose as high as the upstairs bedroom windows of her house. When a slight breeze took hold of it, the bubble really began to rise quickly. It left the cherry tree far behind. It flew above the housetops. It passed over Memorial Park, where some children were playing soccer. It flew over the green hill where her class had gone on a nature walk. It soared above Hart Lake. Ashley was in the air. She was flying her own bubble. She was travelling at last!

She looked back. For just a moment she was afraid. Her garden looked so tiny! Her house, too, looked very small - like a doll's house. And it seemed so far away. The whole village looked tiny.

"Goodness," she said to herself, "now I've done it! I'm leaving! I'm leaving Mom and Dad and Brittany. Oh dear, I'd better be able to get back!"

Suddenly, her doubts and her fears vanished. She began to feel very happy. She had a wonderful feeling that everything would turn out all right. Nothing bad would happen to her. She would not be away from her family for very long. Soon, she would return, but first she would relax and enjoy this great adventure.

She turned towards the sun. She raised her hands high and waved at the white, fleecy clouds. She was in the air at last, and she was very excited about it.

Chapter Three

The bubble was flying smoothly. Far below, Ashley saw a lady galloping a white horse. Ashley loved horses. She wished she was down on the ground right now. The lady might let her ride the beautiful horse. At least she could talk to the lady about horses. She loved to talk about horses.

Suddenly, on her left, Ashley saw the dark smoke of the city. She did not want to go there. That would be dangerous. The city had an airport. Her bubble could not go close to big jets! She closed her eyes tightly and said in a loud voice, "Don't go near the city. Take me far away." She used a very deep voice. It worked. When she opened her eyes, the city was far behind.

She began to think more about her situation. She had to be able to control the bubble. She could not rely on the wind. She would be blown all over the place! She had to fly the bubble. But how?

She began to experiment. First she kept her feet very still and leaned her body to the right. It worked! The bubble began to move to the right. Then she leaned her body to the left. The bubble moved left.

She learned a whole lot of tricks. If she blew gently against the top of the bubble, it climbed higher. If she blew on the floor of the bubble, it moved lower. Blowing in front of her made the bubble go forward. Blowing behind her made the bubble go backwards. This was much easier than she thought it would be!

"Ah, that's better," she said aloud. "I can fly the bubble. I'll just sit down for a few moments and think about where I'm going."

She didn't have time to sit down. Suddenly she heard a whole lot of flapping noises, and shadows covered her bubble. "Eeek!" she shrieked. "Stop it, stop it!!"

Outside the bubble were dozens of tiny birds. They were starlings. There were so many of them that they looked like a big cloud. They were flying all around her. One moment they were beneath her. The next moment they were above her. They were everywhere. They were enjoying themselves a whole lot.

"Oh, please, please, starlings," Ashley cried out, "don't come too close! You'll ruin everything. You'll break my bubble, and I'll fall to the ground."

The little birds took no notice. Like naughty children, they just kept on with their game. Ashley was angry. "You are naughty," she shouted. "Stop this at once!"

To show them how angry she was, she stamped her

foot hard. Oh dear, just for one minute she forgot where she was. Her foot almost went through the bottom of the bubble. She stumbled and fell. As she fell, she pulled her foot back into the bubble.

The starlings took no notice at all. They began to fly faster and faster circles around the bubble, almost touching it with their wings. Ashley panicked. They would break her bubble for sure.

Then she had a bright idea. Her father had taught her to whistle. Not a musical whistle, but the kind of loud whistle you make when you put two fingers in your mouth and blow very hard. It was the whistle she'd heard boys making at soccer games.

"It was naughty of your father to teach you to whistle like that," Ashley's mom had said. "Nice girls don 't do that sort of thing."

Right now, Ashley didn't care whether she was rude or not. She stuck two fingers in her mouth, drew a deep breath and blew as hard as she could.

She even scared herself! Her whistle was really sharp and irritating. It was almost as bad as when Brad Smith scraped his fingernails down the blackboard at school, just to be a pest.

Well, it worked. When the noise came, the birds stopped suddenly, turned and flew away. In a few seconds, there was not a single starling in the sky.

"Oh," Ashley said with a sigh of relief, "thank you

very much, Dad. You really saved my bacon that time!"

Ashley felt a little tired after that excitement. She decided she had to rest. "Whenever you have anything special to do, make sure that you are well rested," Mom used to tell her all the time. Right now that sounded like good advice.

She sat down very carefully on the floor of the bubble. That was not an easy thing to do. Although the bubble looked strong, it was a bubble, and bubbles can break quite easily. The bubble did not break. Also, Ashley found it surprisingly comfortable. It wasn't quite as soft as her pillow at home, but it was quite nice. She folded her arms behind her head and stretched out. "This is good," she said to herself. "I'll have a little nap now." She closed her eyes.

In no time at all, she was wakened up. The sunlight seemed to have vanished. Her head was in a shadow. "What happened?" she asked out loud. She soon knew the answer.

Over her head and right on top of the bubble were four of the biggest, fattest pigeons Ashley had ever seen. Three grey ones and one strange-looking white one. These pigeons were a bigger danger to her than the starlings.

They were playing a game just above her head. They were using her bubble as a slide! They would waddle up the side of the bubble to the very top. Then they would squat down, just as though they were going to ride a toboggan, and they would slide down the bubble and off into the air. Then they would land on the bubble again and walk back up to the top. What fun they were having!

"Oh dear," Ashley said to herself, "what can I do? They are worse than the starlings. They are bigger and heavier. I must get rid of them at once."

She started clapping her hands and shouting loudly, "Shoo, shoo, SHOO." The pigeons did not pay any attention to her.

"Get off my bubble, you naughty creatures!" she cried. "You'll break it with your silly games! Get off NOW!"

It worked. It worked very well, because pigeons are easily scared. They can be stubborn sometimes, but they are not very brave. When Ashley shouted at them, all four rose into the air together and flew away. "Good riddance!" she called after them.

"Oh," Ashley sighed, "what's next? What else can possibly go wrong?"

She looked out through the bubble, trying to find out where she was.

"My goodness!" she squealed. "That's Toronto over there. I can see the CN Tower. This is too much! There are over two million people down there. There are all kinds of tall buildings --- and a huge airport! I'd better get out of here!"

Trying not to panic, she stood with her feet planted firmly on the bottom of the bubble and leaned to her left. The bubble began to move in a wide U-turn, until it was facing the way home. When Ashley blew air gently in front of her, the bubble began to go faster.

She sat down to think about her situation. This trip was definitely dangerous. She could not travel alone like this again. She had to get back home.

“O, there's something else!“ she thought suddenly. “What will I tell my parents? How am I going to explain where I’ve been? I’ve been away for hours!”

Now there was a big problem!

Chapter Four

The bubble flew quickly home. Soon Ashley could see Rosemount below her. Nothing seemed to have changed. The boys were still playing soccer in Memorial Park. Were they the same boys? Ashley shook her head. She was puzzled.

The bubble drifted over her house. There was no one in her garden. She began to have butterflies in her stomach. How was she going to explain her absence? And this bubble?

"I've just got to face the music, I guess," she said to herself. "It will probably be all right, as long as Dad hasn't got himself too worried. He does worry about me sometimes --- even more than Mom does!"

She decided to land near the cherry tree. So she pressed gently on the floor of the bubble and whispered out loud, "Oh, bubble, please land gently!"

Her bubble behaved beautifully. Without even a slight bump, it landed on the grass beside the cherry tree. Ashley looked out to see if anyone had noticed her. No one. She squeezed herself out of the bubble and looked around.

"That's strange," she said in a puzzled voice, "everything looks just the same. There's my stuff for blowing bubbles still on the grass. Yet I have been away for hours."

She looked at her watch. The time was 2:05. "That can't be right," she said. "It was 2:05 when I left. My watch must have stopped."

More problems! She shook her wrist. Her watch must be broken. Then she noticed something else strange. The second hand of her watch was still moving.

"Oh bother!" she said. "Problems, problems, problems! I can't deal with all of this right now. First I'll have to get rid of this bubble."

Ashley walked to the bubble. She would have to destroy it. Trying to explain it to anybody else - especially to Mom and Dad - was impossible. She was just going to break the bubble when she stopped herself.

"Wait a minute," she cried out loud. "What am I doing? I must be crazy! This isn't an ordinary bubble. It's pure magic. I've never had a bubble like this before. I may never have another one like it again. I can't destroy it."

She decided to try something else. She spread her arms out as wide as she could and got hold of the bubble. She began to squeeze it very gently.

It began to get smaller. She pressed it a little more,

and it became even smaller. In a little while, it was only the size of a soccer ball. She picked it up in both hands and began squeezing it the way you do when you make a snowball. In no time at all, the bubble was only the size of an orange.

"What a wonderful bubble you are," Ashley murmured. "You are full of magic. I could not destroy you. I'll keep you and hide you!"

In a corner of the garden was her father's tool shed, where he kept all of his gardening stuff. That would be a great hiding place.

She almost laughed when she looked inside the shed. It was just as she expected --- messy! Dad was great at fixing things, but he was not a neat freak. There was stuff all over the place. Tools were leaning against the walls. A broken wheelbarrow was upside down on the floor. The shelves were filled with boxes of nails and screws, balls of string, paint cans and old plant pots.

"This is great," Ashley said. "Just what I need. I'll put my precious bubble inside one of these plant pots. Nobody will ever know it's there."

She dragged an old kitchen chair from a corner and reached up to the bottom shelf. She chose a small pot and popped the bubble inside.

When she had finished, she picked up her bubble-blowing stuff from the garden and went into the house. As soon as she got in, Dad called out to her.

“Well, you didn’t stay out very long, young lady. What’s the matter? Were the bugs biting you?”

Ashley didn’t answer right away. She was too surprised. She glanced quickly at the kitchen clock. It said 2:20. Gosh, according to the clock and according to her watch, she hadn’t been out in the garden very long. What had happened to the time? Could it have been standing still all the time she was in the bubble?

“Oh, sorry, Dad,” she said at last. “I didn’t mean to bother you. I forgot my thermos of lemonade. I came back for it. I’m going out again.” She didn’t want to tell a lie, but she thought that this time a little lie would be better than the truth. Of course, she knew that even little lies are still lies. As her mom said, “Lies are lies, my dear, no matter what size they are. There are no such things as little lies!” Mom had a lot of sayings like that! Maybe all moms had.

As her dad walked into the kitchen, he gave her a very strange look. “Ashley,” he said, “you’re really weird. Your thermos isn’t in the house. I saw you take it into the garden only half an hour ago. You just don’t seem to have your head screwed on right today!”

“Oh, I’m sorry, Dad. My fault again. I thought I had left the lemonade inside. I guess my head has been in the clouds or something.”

As soon as she said that, Ashley could have bitten her tongue. Of all the things to say, that was the dumbest! But she was smiling to herself. It was funny when you thought about it. Her head sure had been in the clouds!

"I don't know where your head was, Ashley," her father. "I do know that I'd like you to start using it!"

"Hey, Dad, you're making up a lot of jokes, aren't you? I didn't know you were a comedian!" she replied. "I guess I'll just have to head out into the garden!" She laughed when she said this. Her dad and she often had jokes together. They both had what you might call a weird sense of humour.

"Ashley," her dad laughed, "whatever did I do to deserve such a crazy daughter! Out you go, before you wake up your sister!"

Ashley went back into the garden. There was the thermos of lemonade, right in front of her. Oh, no! Now she realised she had left her bubble-making kit inside the house. She would not go back for it. She didn't want to blow any more bubbles today. What she needed most of all right now was time to think.

She lay down on the grass and closed her eyes. She would have to think carefully. She had plans to make. First of all, she had to tell somebody about the bubble. She couldn't keep it a complete secret.

She decided to tell Stephanie and Kristine. After all, they were her very best friends. Unfortunately, she would have to wait until tomorrow ... but she could hardly wait for tomorrow to come!

Chapter Five

The next morning, the three friends gathered in Ashley's garden. She had hardly slept all night. She had dreamed about flying high above the clouds --- though the bubble couldn't actually go that high!

"Oh," Kristine groaned, "what time is it anyway? It feels like five o'clock in the morning. Ashley, why did you drag us out of bed so early?"

"Stop being silly," Stephanie snapped. "It's 9.30, for heaven's sake. That's not so early!"

"Huh!" Kristine replied, "I'm more awake than you two. See what I can do so early in the morning."

She got up from the grass and began doing cartwheels all over the place. One, two, three, four, five ..... beside the cherry tree, down by the tool shed, in front of Mrs. Miller's favourite flower bed. Ashley had dreadful visions of Kristine landing in the middle of the roses.

"Please, Kristine," she called out, "please stop. Come back and sit down with us. I've got something important to tell you. But I can't tell you if you're going to go ape on me."

"Okay," Kristine said with a grin, "I'll stop. I know what you want me to do. Like the beekeeper said to the bee, you want me to 'bee-hive' myself!" She burst out laughing. "I made that one up myself," she said. "Not bad, eh?"

Stephanie and Ashley groaned. "It's too early for your jokes," they said together. "Come and sit down."

Kristine came and sat with them again, but she still wasn't quiet. "I was just buzzing around a little," she said, "but I didn't mean to be a bumble bee."

"Kristine, sometimes you are not funny at all," Ashley said seriously. "You shouldn't joke when we are trying to be serious."

Ashley was a very honest girl. She always said what was on her mind. Kristine settled down right away.

Stephanie was a little impatient. "Please, Ashley," she said, "tell us why you asked us to come here. I'm very busy, you know. What did you want to tell us?"

"First, I have to show you something," Ashley replied. "Then I'll do lots of talking, believe me - and you will, too!"

She led them to the shed. Once inside, she climbed onto the kitchen chair and took down the plant pot.

"There," she announced, "there's what I wanted to show you."

Stephanie and Kristine looked into the plant pot. They

were silent for a few moments. Kristine was the first to speak.

"A soap bubble! Ashley, are you losing your marbles?" she asked.

Stephanie was frowning. She examined the bubble for a long time.

"I can see what it is," she said. "It's a bubble. A soap bubble. An ordinary bubble. Is THAT the reason you brought us here?"

She did not sound pleased. In fact, she sounded just like Mrs. Wallis, their teacher, who had a cold, frosty voice when she was unhappy about something.

Kristine tried to make things a little better. "I know what this is all about, Ashley. It's laundry day at your house. You want to show us what kind of detergent you're using," she joked.

Ashley smiled. "Come outside for a minute," she said. "I'll show you something that will really surprise you." She led her friends over to the cherry tree. That's where the magic had begun for her.

"Now watch carefully." She gently tipped the bubble from the plant pot until it rolled into the palm of her hand. Then she raised her hand and blew softly.

The bubble floated into the air. Then Ashley blew on it again ...... and the bubble grew bigger! Once, twice, three times she blew. Each time the bubble was bigger. Soon it was now the size of a small bush. It settled down on the grass beside Ashley.

Kristine was clapping her hands and jumping up and down with excitement. Stephanie was a lot calmer, but her eyes were shining.

"Ashley," Stephanie said, "you have to explain this to us. Is it a trick you read about in a book? I know you read a lot -"

"No," Ashley interrupted, "it's not a trick. Well, not the way you mean it, anyway. It's not something I read about either. It just happened - right here - yesterday. And there's lots more to it, too. Let me tell you all about it."

She did tell them. She told them where the bubble had come from. And she told them about the strange journey she had taken. But the part that astonished them most of all was what happened after she returned home --- time had stood still, and no one had known that she had been away.

When Ashley finished, her friends were amazed. Kristine couldn't even think of a joke to make. Stephanie was puzzled.

"Now let me make sure I understand this," Stephanie said. "We have this bubble --- this one right here --- which can become big enough to carry people and small enough to be hidden in a plant pot. And this bubble --- this one right here --- can be flown, just like an aeroplane, wherever you want to go. Have I got it right?"

"That's exactly right," Ashley replied. "I can go wherever I like in this bubble, and nobody even knows that

I've been away."

"Boy, oh boy," Kristine interrupted. "Nobody's gonna believe this. They'll think we're really crazy. Yikes, I don't think we should tell anybody anything!"

"This is going to take a lot of thought," Stephanie said quietly. "It's no ordinary thing, you know. It could change our whole lives."

Ashley smiled. "That's why I asked you over here this morning. It's too important to keep to myself. I need your help with it. Of course, I don't want to go on any more trips alone. No way!"

Stephanie became quite excited. "It's really fantastic! Do you realise that we can travel ANYWHERE? We can go wherever we want to go! And now, we don't need a book or a computer to find it out stuff. We can just climb into the bubble and get the information for ourselves!"

Kristine began dancing with joy. She was almost going to start turning cartwheels again, but Ashley stopped her.

Ashley spoke very calmly to her friends, because she was a very sensible girl. "Don't you want to test the bubble before we do anything else? It worked for me yesterday, but perhaps you should try it for yourselves first."

"We don't need to do that, Ashley," Kristine burst out. "You don't have to prove anything. We believe you."

"What we need most," Stephanie added calmly, "is organisation. This is important business. We have to get organised."

"Wow!" said Kristine "you mean we're going to organise an Air Force, or something? Oh, I like that." She was rolling her eyes and laughing. "Bubble Power," she said, "I'm all for Bubble Power!"

"Kristine, stop making jokes!" Ashley said. "Stephanie is right. We have to get organised. There is work to do. We have to organise flights and timetables. All kinds of stuff has to be done. And I've got a good suggestion about how to start."

Her friends listened carefully. Ashley usually had good ideas.

"I think," Ashley said, "that we ought to form a club."

"Awesome!" her friends shouted. "A great idea! We need a club!"

They sat down together on the grass, right beside the bubble. Their first problem was a name for the club.

"How about The Rosemount Flying Club?" Ashley asked her friends. "We live in Rosemount, so it seems like a good name."

"I'm not sure about the 'Flying Club' part," Stephanie said. "It sounds too much like a club for adults. Why not call it The Junior Explorers Club? After all, that's what we intend to do - explore."

"You guys," groaned Kristine, "you're so boring! They are really boring names. Remember, our aeroplane is a soap bubble. So we've got to mention that. And we're going to be flying a lot, so the flying club thing sounds okay to me. I've got a great name for us." She looked at her friends and grinned from ear to ear. "Ready?" she continued. "Here it is - THE SOAPY SUDS FLYING CLUB!"

Ashley and Stephanie burst out laughing. Once they started, they couldn't stop. They laughed and laughed until tears were rolling down their cheeks.

"Oh, Kristine," Stephanie said, "you're crazy ... but sometimes you're very funny, too. I think that name's crazy enough to be the right one. Besides, nobody will ever know, from that name, just what we're up to. I vote for The Soapy Suds Flying Club!"

And so, that very morning, in Ashley's Miller's garden, The Soapy Suds Flying Club was born. The three friends decided that their club would be quite different from all other clubs. They wouldn't have a President and a Secretary and a Treasurer, and so on. They organised it as a proper flying club. Stephanie drew up the list, as follows:

Chief Pilot:	Ashley Miller
Navigator:	Stephanie Brewer
Observer:	Kristine Kelly.

Ashley was elected Chief Pilot because the bubble belonged to her, and also she knew how to fly it. Stephanie became the Navigator, because the navigator had to be good at reading maps. She was very good at that. Kristine was made Observer because she had really good eyesight. She never missed anything that was going on. It was her job to watch out for danger ... especially starlings and pigeons!

When these decisions had been made, the three friends were a little tired of serious discussions.

"I want to get started," Kristine said. "I want to DO something. All this talk has tired me out."

"What do you think, Ashley?" Stephanie asked. "Do you think we could be ready to take a trip soon?"

"Ready!" Ashley responded. "Ready! I'm ready to go this very minute. How about you two?"

"Just hold on," Stephanie replied, "we've got things to do first. It's almost lunchtime. So we should have our lunch. Then I could get my maps and notebooks from home. You, Kristine, could borrow your father's binoculars. And you, Ashley, could get a radio and maybe some sandwiches for us. Then - just listen to this! - we could take our very first trip this afternoon."

Ashley and Kristine thought that was a great idea. They all went home to have a quick lunch and to collect the things they needed. The Soapy Suds Flying Club was taking off!

Chapter Six

The first meeting of the Soapy Suds Flying Club was held after lunch in Ashley Miller's garden. The first meeting almost didn't take place at all.

"We forgot to put the bubble away when we went to have lunch," Ashley said. "Anything might have happened. The wind might have carried it away. Or my dad might have found it."

"You're quite right," Stephanie replied. "Look after the bubble. That should be our first rule"

"Yeah, right," chimed in Kristine. "After all, without the bubble we're nothing. No bubble, no club."

"Now that's taken care of," said Ashley, "let's see if we've got our flight organised. Stephanie, did you get the maps?"

"Yes, I did," Stephanie said. "It was a little difficult, because we have the whole world to choose from. Of course, I didn't have maps for everywhere! So I chose the maps that would get us to Japan."

"Japan!" exclaimed Kristine. "Did you say Japan?

Do you realise just how far away that is? We'll never get there before suppertime!"

"Don't be so silly," burst out Ashley. "With our bubble, we'll get there in no time at all! Besides, Japan is a very interesting country. I've always wanted to see Tokyo. What a great place for our first trip. Well done, Stephanie."

Kristine rolled her eyes, but she didn't say any more. Maybe she shouldn't have been so quick to criticise, but sometimes Ashley and Stephanie could be ... well, sometimes you would think they were thirty-four years old, or something!

"I got my little radio from my bedroom," Ashley continued, "but I couldn't make us any sandwiches, or stuff like that. Mom was in the kitchen the whole time. She would have blown a fuse if I'd walked out with a big bag of food. But I did manage to get bubble gum ... lots of it. We'll enjoy that."

"Here are the binoculars," Kristine added. "Dad thinks I'm going birdwatching. Not very likely, I'd say, because I can't tell one bird from another! At least I know what starlings and pigeons look like. That should be enough."

Stephanie stood up and looked at her friends. "That's it," she said. "We're ready. Let's do it."

"Let's go," Ashley echoed. She had a very serious look on her face. "But we must start properly. Let's form a circle, with our hands on each other's shoulders." She waited until her friends had done what she suggested.

"Good, then we must all say together: 'One for all, and all for one!' That will be our club motto."

They did just as Ashley said. Under the cherry tree, they chanted together: "One for all, and all for one!"

Then Ashley blew gently on the shiny bubble until it was big enough to hold all of them.

"Now," she told them, "just do as I do --- but be very gentle."

She squeezed herself carefully into the bubble. Then she asked her friends to follow. Stephanie went in first and then Kristine. When they got inside, they were very excited.

"Lift off!" Ashley cried. "The Soapy Suds Flying Club is into lift off. Over and out!" When she had said that, she blew gently upwards. The bubble trembled like a leaf - and then it began to rise in the air!

First it rose until it was just over the cherry tree. Then it was as high as the rooftop. Soon it was above the houses and tall trees. It flew very quickly over the green hill where a family was having a picnic on the grass. It passed over Memorial Park, where some adults were playing tennis. Soon Rosemount was far behind.

The three friends had to work very hard. Ashley was busy controlling the bubble, steering it on a straight path. Stephanie was studying her maps carefully. Kristine was using the binoculars, looking for starlings and pigeons.

"We're okay now," Ashley announced. "We're flying smoothly. Now there's only one problem. Which way is

Japan?"

Stephanie was a big help. "I think I've got it figured out, Ashley," she said. "We just have to choose which way we want to go. We can go east, or we can go west. If we go east, we have to cross the Atlantic Ocean. If we go west, we fly across Canada and the Pacific. Flying west is probably shorter. What do you prefer?"

"I'd like to go west," Kristine said. "I've been east with my parents. We went to see Ann of Green Gables last year. You know ...... on Prince Edward Island. But I've never been out west. That's the way I'd like to go."

"There's another point to consider too," Ashley observed. "If we go west, we'll be going with the sun. So we'll have a lot more hours of daylight for flying. After all, when it's two o'clock in the afternoon in Rosemount, it's still only eleven in the morning in British Columbia. I think we should travel west."

"Good, that's settled," Stephanie said. "Let's go west!"

Ashley brought the bubble around till it was facing west. "We're on course, navigator!" she announced. "Japan, here we come!"

With those words, Kristine became so excited that she started jumping up and down. "Hooray, hooray!" she cried, "we're on our way. No more delay! Let's go today! This is pure poetry!"

Ashley and Stephanie were horrified. The bubble was

bouncing up and down as Kristine jumped with her hands held high over her head."

"Kristine!" they shouted together. "Stop! Stop right now. You'll break the bubble!"

Too late. The floor of the bubble was all right. But one of Kristine's hands pushed right through the roof of the bubble.

"Oh," groaned Ashley, "look, there's a hole. Our bubble is wrecked!"

Three pairs of eyes looked up as a small hole appeared in the bubble, right over their heads. There was a hissing sound as air began escaping from . Worse still, the hole began to get larger and larger. It was soon as big as a baseball.

Kristine was so ashamed of what she had done that she began to cry. Ashley could only stare at the dangerous hole. She was so disappointed that the great dream seemed to be over.

Stephanie came to the rescue. "Don't panic," she said. "Whatever you do, don't panic." She turned to Ashley. "Quick, get out that bubble gum you brought."

Ashley's eyes were round with astonishment. "Bubble gum!" she exclaimed. "How can you think of bubble gum at a time like this! Why ---"

"Don't waste time," Stephanie cried.

The bubble was beginning to shake a little. It began to fall ever so gradually. Something had to be done quickly, or the bubble would crash!.

Stephanie grabbed several coloured balls of bubble gum from Ashley's hand. She stuffed some of them into her mouth and began to chew. She gave some to Kristine and Ashley. "Come on, you two," she said, "chew as much gum as you can. Quickly now! We haven't much time."

Her two friends didn't know what was going on, but they, too, began to chew.

After a moment, they were stopped by a shout from Stephanie. "Ashley!" she cried out, "where on earth did you get this bubble gum? It's sour! It's the sourest bubble gum I've ever had!"

"Ugh," agreed Kristine, "this is worse than eatingbroccoli. It's terrible."

"Oh dear, I'm sorry," Ashley said. "I didn't know it was like this. I've never had it before. It's new stuff my dad bought for me."

"I wouldn't give this to my worst enemy," Stephanie, screwing her eyes tight shut as she chewed.

"Worst enemy?" Kristine laughed, "That's a great idea! When we get back, remind me to give some of this gum to Amy Fisher."

"Amy Fisher?" Ashley asked. "What's wrong with Amy Fisher?"

"Don't you know?" Stephanie groaned. "Amy Fisher really thinks she's somebody. She's always hanging around the door of the staffroom at school. She's always asking the teachers if they have any stuff they want her to do for them."

"If not Amy Fisher," Kristine continued, "I'd give a whole pile of this awful gum to Brad Smith. He deserves it!"

"Brad?" Ashley questioned. "Why Brad?"

"Because he's bad. BAD Brad, I call him. Besides, he's a boy," Kristine replied. "He deserves this gum because he's a boy!"

"He can't help that," Ashley said. "He can't help being a boy. You can't criticize him for that. It's not his fault!"

"Never mind that now," Stephanie interrupted. "We've got an emergency on our hands. Chew the gum. Hurry!"

They chewed gum. They chewed lots of gum. They chewed, even though their eyes were watering with the sour taste.

"Okay. Here comes the icky part," Stephanie said at last. "Give me the gum you've chewed." Stephanie took their gum and added it to the gum from her own mouth. She worked it all together, just as though she was mixing a cake or something. Then she flattened it out until it was about the size of a sheet of paper.

"There, that ought to do the trick," she said. She placed the sheet of gum carefully over the hole in the bubble. "Help me hold it in place," she asked, "until it sticks properly to the bubble. It's got to seal the hole completely."

Three pairs of hands held the patch in place. No more air was escaping. The hole was not getting any bigger. In fact, you couldn't see the hole any more. It was completely covered by the gum.

"Wow," Kristine said with a sigh of relief, "you fixed the problem, Stephanie. Thank goodness! That's the biggest band-aid I've ever seen."

Ashley giggled. "What a crazy idea," she said. "But, in a way, it was absolutely the right thing to do ---- a bubble gum patch for a bubble! What could be better? You're really smart, Stephanie."

The danger was over, and the three friends were able to relax. They could laugh at what had happened. Of course, they had all been afraid --- but they weren't about to admit that! When Ashley was had got the bubble flying smoothly again, she turned to her friends and offered them good advice.

"It's going to be a long flight, and we've had a lot of excitement. I think we'd better have a good rest."

Kristine and Stephanie agreed. The three travellers stretched out on the floor of the bubble and closed their eyes.

"I'll just find some nice, soft music on the radio," Ashley added. "Then things will be perfect."

The girls drifted off to sleep as music filled the bubble. Perfect peace, but not for long ......

Chapter Seven

They were woken up suddenly only thirty minutes later. A huge noise got them awake in a hurry.

"Ooohhh," shrieked Kristine, "help! Something awful is happening!"

Ashley and Stephanie jumped up too. As usual, Ashley tried to calm everyone down.

"Okay, okay," she said, "keep calm, Kristine. Nothing bad is going to happen. Let's see what is going on."

Stephanie rolled her eyes. She could hardly hear her friend's voice because of all the banging and crashing that was going on right outside.

It was a terrible thunderstorm. The noise was deafening, and the sky was black.

The music on the radio had stopped, and a man was talking. "There's a major storm warning for this area," he said. "Thunderstorms and lightning have already arrived. There may also be tornadoes."

"Switch that off!" Kristine called out. "I don't want to hear it!"

"Suddenly there was more thunder. The girls were so scared that they bumped into one another. They huddled together in the middle of the bubble. Kristine was almost crying. Stephanie was a white as a sheet. Ashley was trying hard to stay calm.

"Come on," she said at last, "let's sit down and relax. We've seen lots of thunderstorms before. This one is no different. Let's sit down and wait for it to pass."

She surprised herself. Inside, she was really frightened. Her heart was pounding. If she'd been at home, in her own bed, she would have hidden under the bedclothes. Now she was trying to handle this situation really well.

Kristine and Stephanie managed to settle down. Then things got worse suddenly. The whole sky seemed to catch fire.

"Lightning! Oh no, not lightning!" Kristine shouted. Stephanie jumped like a frightened rabbit. Ashley's face was absolutely white..

They were in the middle of a huge storm. The noise was terrifying. It was all around them. Lightning flashed past their bubble, like jet planes at an air show.

Ashley was brave. "It's all right," she said. "Sit down here. The storm will pass. Pretty soon it will be over, and we'll be able to laugh about it." Stephanie and Kristine became a lot more calm.

"Of course," Stephanie said, "a thunderstorm is nothing really. I did a school project on thunderstorms.

Remember? Thunderstorms are just a lot of hot air which gets a bit out of control." She tried to laugh about it.

Kristine tried to be brave also. She gave a little laugh.

"Yes," she said, "There's nothing to be afraid of. This noise isn't as bad as the noise my Dad makes when he's clearing away the dishes after dinner!"

"We should have known this would happen," Ashley said. "After all, it's July, and we're over the prairies right now. There are a lot of summer thunderstorms in the prairies.

"I know what we should do," Stephanie said after a few moments. "We should sing a song. Remember the songs we learned last summer, when we went to camp together?"

Kristine smiled. "I remember. It was great! Sitting round the campfire every night and singing. I loved it."

"Great idea," said Ashley. "And I know just the song to sing. Do you remember 'Everywhere we go'? All we have to do is to change the words a little bit, and we'll have our own song."

What happened was strange. Three girls floating in a bubble, a long, long way from home ------ and they were singing. They were singing loudly. They were singing so loudly that they were red in the face! What a brave song it was. It was a song which they would never forget ... ever!

Everywhere we go-o,
Everywhere we go-o,
People always ask us,
People always ask us,
Who-oo we are, are
Who-oo we are, are.
So we always tell them,
So we always tell them,
We are the Flying Club,
We are the Flying Club..
Then they always ask us
Then they always ask us,
Can you sing it louder?
Can you sing it louder?
So we always tell them,
So we always tell them,
If you want it louder,
If you want it louder,
WE ARE THE FLYING CLUB,
THE SOAPY SUDS FLYING CLUB!

The song ended in wild laughter. They forgot that they were frightened. They forgot about danger. They rolled around on the floor of the bubble, laughing.

Chapter Eight

Suddenly the laughter stopped.

"Just a minute, you guys," Kristine shouted. "There's something wrong. There's a big puddle of water on the floor!"

"Impossible," Ashley snapped. "We didn't bring any water into the bubble. How can there be water here?"

"Oh, look up there for a minute." It was Stephanie. She was pointing to the roof of the bubble. There was a very tiny leak. Rain was dripping slowly into the bubble.

"I can't take any more of this," Ashley groaned. "When are the problems going to stop? I don't know how to solve this one."

Stephanie replied quickly, shouting above the noise of the storm. "Don't worry about this one. I'll take care of it."

She opened up a small canvas bag she had brought with her. Ashley and Kristine were surprised. They hadn't noticed the bag before.

Stephanie began pulling things out of the bag. First

there was a packet of tissues. Then there was a small mirror. Then there was a toothbrush and a tube of toothpaste. Next came a nail file. It was followed by a pair of tweezers and a brush and a comb. Soon there was a little heap of things lying on the floor.

"Stephanie, what is going on here?" Kristine asked. She was angry. "All you ever think about is how you look. We're drowning - and you're looking for your comb! You're crazy!"

Ashley was upset, too. "Stephanie, why you did you bring all that junk with you.? Put it away. We've got a serious problem!"

Stephanie paid no attention to them. She just kept searching in her bag. At last she brought out the last thing in the bag. It was --- a small can of hair spray!

Ashley and Kristine groaned. "No, don't be like that," Stephanie said. "This will solve the problem. Watch!"

She stood up and began to spray the roof of the balloon. She sprayed it very well. She did not miss a single centimeter.

Ashley and Kristine watched her silently. They thought this was awesome. Their eyes were as round as saucers with astonishment.

Stephanie's trick worked! The leak stopped.

"That is some trick," Kristine exclaimed. "How did you think of it?"

"Well, this is a special kind of hair spray," Stephanie

said. “It’s a really strong .... oh, what do you call it? .... oh, bother .... oh, yes. That’s it. It’s a really strong lacquer.”

Ashley began to laugh. “It’s funny, really,” she said, “because I thought you were only concerned about brushing your hair. You’re always combing your hair or cleaning your teeth or painting your nails, or something!”

“That’s right,” Kristine agreed. “You’re the only one who brought a toothbrush on this trip. I don’t know how you remember that stuff!”

Now that the bubble wasn’t going to be flooded, they enjoyed the joke together. The storm still raged on. The thunder was still noisy. The lightning flashed. But they were not afraid. Their friendship made them strong.

Then, without warning, disaster struck again. The bubble had been flying smoothly, in spite of the strong winds outside. But everything changed quickly.

The bubble began to spin around. Round and round it went, picking up speed, until it looked like a ride at an amusement park. The three girls shrieked together. They were all scared.

“Put your hands against the walls,” Ashley shouted, “and put your feet firmly on the floor. You don’t want to be thrown out!”

“This isn’t funny any more,” Kristine squealed. “This time we’ve really had it!”

“We’re in big trouble,” Stephanie shouted. “We’re on the edge of a tornado. We’re going to spin right into the middle of it."

She was right. A huge black cloud had suddenly appeared. It was shaped like a funnel and it reached almost to the ground. The noise was louder than a hundred diesel trains!

This was real danger! Ashley knew that she would have to act quickly.

"Quickly," she ordered her friends. "come to my side of the bubble. We've got to stand together at this spot. And we've got to put all of our weight in this direction. The tornado is on the other side. So if we lean hard here, there's a chance we might be able to push the bubble away from the funnel. Come on, do it now, before it's too late!"

She didn't need to say another word. Stephanie and Kristine joined her at once. Together, they leaned against the side of the bubble, pushing as hard as they could.

The bubble began to bounce up and down like a yo-yo. They were pushing it one way, and the tornado was pulling it the opposite way. The girls were shaken so much that they almost lost their balance. But they held on. They kept pushing and pushing.

"It's working, it's working," Stephanie called out. "See, we've moved a little away from the funnel cloud!"

"Don't stop pushing," Ashley replied. "We're not clear of the tornado yet. Come on. Push! Harder! Push!"

A strange thing happened. The bubble had been spinning in circles around the funnel cloud, but it broke free very suddenly. It did not float away gently. It broke away from the black cloud with amazing force. It snapped away like a rubber band and sped across the sky.

It flew so fast that they suddenly found themselves in bright sunshine. They had been flung far beyond the storm, which was now a long way away.

"Hip, hip, hooray!" Kristine shouted. "I never thought I'd be glad to have such pushy friends." She giggled at her own joke.

Ashley and Stephanie enjoyed the joke, too. They were relieved. They were ready to laugh. They deserved a good laugh!

With smiles on their faces, they looked out happily at the blue sky and the fleecy, white clouds.

"It's a lovely day," Ashley murmured, "a lovely day."

"And it's going to be even lovelier," Stephanie said. "Look what's ahead of us. See? Ahead of us? It's the Rocky Mountains!"

They were thrilled at the sight. They had never seen such high mountains. The mountain tops were decorated with white snow, even now, in the month of July.

It was all so beautiful that they could not speak. They stared and stared. At that moment, they had no regrets at all. This was going to be a wonderful trip.

Chapter Nine

They drifted smoothly through the Rockies. There were white clouds high over their heads. Not far below, there were green forests as far as the eye could see.

"I wonder how many bears are down there, among the trees," Kristine said.

"Lots, I'm sure," Stephanie remarked. She was writing in her journal and didn't appreciate being interrupted. "Why don't you use your binoculars to try to see some?"

"Too many trees," Kristine replied. "I've never seen so many trees. You could never find a bear down there."

Ashley sighed. "After all the excitement, it seems kind of quiet now. What are you so busy with, Stephanie?"

"I'm writing in my journal," Stephanie said. "I write in my journal every day."

"A journal?" Kristine asked. She made a funny face as she continued: "What's a journal? I didn't know you had a journal. What is it?"

"It's just a kind of diary," Ashley explained. "It's like keeping a diary."

"I wish I'd brought something to do," Ashley observed. "I should have brought a book or something. I like to read. I wish I had a book with me."

"You and your books," Kristine laughed. "I bet you've read maybe a hundred books. I'm glad you didn't bring them all with you. The bubble would never have got off the ground!"

"I've read over four hundred books." Ashley replied seriously. "And not just picture books. I've read dozens and dozens of chapter books. I like chapter books most of all."

"Oh, I loved that one you lent to me," Stephanie said. "Remember? 'Lisa Long, Paper Girl'. It was about a girl who couldn't get a job delivering newspapers, because everybody said that was a boy's job."

"Yes," Ashley agreed, "and her father had to phone the newspaper office and make them give her a newspaper route. When she got the job, she proved she was better than any of the boys. She signed up a whole lot of new readers for the paper --"

"And she won first prize in the sales competition," Stephanie chimed in, " .... a new bicycle. Now that's what I call a good story."

"Can you imagine how the boys would feel if that happened in Rosemount?" Kristine asked, with a grin. "I bet they would turn green! We should try it sometime. It would serve them right!"

Ashley smiled. "It would be quite a joke, wouldn't it? The boys in Rosemount don't exactly believe in women's liberation ---"

Her words were cut off suddenly. "Look!" Stephanie called out. "Over there ...... just ahead. It's the ocean. It's the Pacific Ocean!"

"The Pacific! Great!" Kristine had a big grin on her face. "I've seen the Atlantic Ocean, and now I'm seeing the Pacific."

It was great. It was so huge and so blue. Big, blue waves, with white tops on them, were rolling towards the shore.

Kristine snatched up her binoculars again and looked over the shoreline. "Hey, you won't believe this," she exclaimed. "Over there. On the rocks. There, that little island. Look!" She pushed the binoculars at Ashley as she spoke.

It was Ashley's turned to be impressed. "Sea lions," she said, her voice filled with excitement. "I've never seen sea lions before ... and so many of them!"

"Let me see," Stephanie asked. She studied the creatures on the rocks below. "That's a whole family, I think. I can see the male ... I think he's called the bull, or something."

"That's awful big for one family, isn't it?" Kristine commented. "There must be at least a dozen of them down there."

"Well, the male usually has a big family," Stephanie explained. "He has more than one mate."

"Hm, I don't think I approve of that." Ashley had a strong sense of what was right. "It doesn't sound fair at all."

"Animals are different from humans," Stephanie said. "You shouldn't judge their behaviour by our behaviour."

Ashley shrugged her shoulders and concentrated on flying the bubble. As they floated out over open water, they were not going quite so smoothly. Small air currents were making their flight a little bumpy. She had to be alert in case of problems.

The sea lion's family began to make her think of her own family. She was beginning to miss Mom and Dad and little Brittany. What were they doing right now, she wondered. Her baby sister was probably eating again. Another bottle! She loved her formula!

Her thoughts were interrupted by Kristine, who was all excited again.

"You've just GOT to see this," she was saying. "How lucky can you get? Look down there!"

Just to their left, there were five or six whales floating on the surface of the ocean. They were relaxed, rather like sunbathers at the beach.

"Blue whales!" Ashley's eyes were big and round. "I never thought that I'd ever see a blue whale ...... not in a million years!"

“How do you know that they’re blue whales?” Kristine asked.

“Their size, for a start,” Ashley replied. “Just look at them. They’re huge. Actually, they are the biggest creatures on the earth.’

‘That’s right,” agreed Stephanie. “One of those whales down there probably weighs more than a thousand people.”

“Oh, look! One of them is starting to blow water out of the top of its head. Wow! that’s quite a shower head!” Kristine was really impressed.

“It’s not blowing water,” Stephanie explained. “It’s breathing. It’s blowing air. It looks like steam, because of condensation.”

“Who needs an encyclopedia with you guys around!” Kristine was chuckling. She didn’t mind that Ashley and Stephanie knew so much about whales. After all, she knew about other things, like dinosaurs. She knew more about dinosaurs than anybody else did. “Anyway,” she added, with a grin, “I’m glad I don’t have a hole like that in the top of my head!”

Ashley corrected her. “In a way you do have. You see, it’s not just any old hole. It’s a nostril. As a matter of fact, that’s one way you can identify a blue whale. Like the humpback whale, and some others, it has two nostrils.”

Stephanie would not be outdone. “That’s correct,” she agreed. “Some whales only have one nostril.”

“I wonder why that is?” Kristine asked. “Why aren’t

all whales the same?"

Ashley and Stephanie were enjoying themselves now. They loved sharing their knowledge. "There are two main species of whales," Ashley explained. "There are ---"

Kristine couldn't take any more of this. "Okay already!" she said. "I just asked one little question. I don't need a whole speech, you know. You two are worse than my mom and dad!"

She was cut off by a shout from Stephanie. "They're starting to move. There must be a whole school of them ...... that's what their groups are called - schools ... or pods."

The whales were obviously feeling good. Some of them were jumping right out of the water and leaping into the air.

"That's awesome," Ashley sighed. "Unbelievable," whispered Stephanie.

"They're having a whale of a time," chuckled Kristine.

Groaning, Ashley and Stephanie screwed up their faces. Kristine never gave up with the bad jokes.

The whales were moving off at high speed. Soon they were no more than tiny specks in the blue ocean. Seeing them had been unforgettable.

Chapter Ten

"Land, land ahoy!" Stephanie called out. "Quickly now, I think we've reached Japan!"

Her friends looked out eagerly. Kristine was peering through the binoculars "Land?" she said. "I don't see any land. There's only water ...... lots and lots of water."

"You've got to look in the right direction," Ashley observed quietly. "Right now you're looking straight down at the ocean."

"Ugh!" grunted Kristine. She was embarrassed. She hated to look foolish. "These binoculars are hard to use, you know," she grumbled.

Just ahead was a group of islands. They stretched out over the ocean like a long necklace.

"There are four main islands," Stephanie said. "Let's steer a little to the right. That should bring us to the main island. Tokyo, the capital city, is on the main island."

The bubble moved to the right. "Help me get more speed," Ashley asked her friends. "Blow gently forward. Oh, good! It's moving beautifully."

They reached land quickly. They were soon flying quite low over the largest city they had ever seen.

"Tokyo!" Kristine shrieked with excitement. "It's Tokyo!"

The girls couldn't help themselves. They were clapping their hands, and they were laughing. But their joy ended suddenly.

"Wait a minute!" Ashley shouted. "What's happening?"

They were surrounded. On all sides of the bubble there were very strange creatures bobbing up and down. They were like ghosts as they came into sight suddenly and then, just as suddenly, disappeared. There were dozens of them, and they were very, very strange. There were scary dragons and fierce-looking warriors and huge long fishes and shiny flying machines that were much bigger than the bubble.

By now, Kristine was clinging to Ashley, whose eyes were wide open with astonishment.

Stephanie was the first to take charge of the situation. "Don't panic," she said. "Ashley, take the bubble up higher. Quickly now. We've got to get out of this - fast!"

Kristine had dropped the binoculars. She had her eyes covered. "I don't want to see this," she cried. "Are these things from outer space, or what? I hope we didn't get to Mars by mistake."

"Calm down," her friend replied. "You don't need to

hide your eyes. They're just kites. We're surrounded by kites. Yes, that's all they are ...... KITES!"

Stephanie was right. They were kites. Dozens of kites. Dozens of very strange kites. They filled the sky all around the bubble.

Ashley flew the bubble higher. In a few moments, the kites, still bobbing in the air, were far below them.

"I forgot. I read about it in the guide book. I should have told you. The Japanese are very fond of kites," Stephanie said with a smile.

"I've never seen kites like those in the store," Kristine exclaimed.

"They are beautiful," observed Ashley. "They are so colourful and so big - and they fly so well."

"Yes," Stephanie agreed, "...... and you know what? Families make their own kites. Everybody joins in - the parents and the children. They spend weeks making one kite. Then everybody goes out to a park to fly the kite. I read that there are even kite competitions, with hundreds of people taking part."

"I can believe that," Kristine exclaimed. "Look at all those people down there in the park. But, you know, they could have killed us with their kites. If a kite had crashed into the bubble - oh boy ...."

"It's not their fault," Ashley said. "Haven't you realised by now that they can't see us - or the bubble. We can see them, but they can't see us ...... not until we step outside the bubble, that is."

"Isn't that cool!" remarked Stephanie. "Well, I don't know about you two, but I need some exercise. Why don't we land now? The park looks pretty nice. We could land down there and pay a visit."

"You've got my vote," said Kristine. "Let's hit the brakes!"

Ashley rolled her eyes. Sometimes Kristine could be a bit weird. "Okay, you're both right," she declared. "It's time to go down. Concentrate really hard and we'll bring the bubble down."

The three friends guided the bubble towards the park below them. They steered away from the huge crowd of people who were flying the kites.

"That's it," Ashley cried. "Over there, behind those tall bushes. But be careful - we don't want any branches to burst the bubble."

It was a perfect landing. The bubble simply floated gently to the ground. They were behind a very tall hedge. No one could see them.

"Be very careful as you get out of the bubble," Ashley warned her friends. "Don't break it. We need it to fly home again."

They did what she said. They squeezed out of the bubble very carefully.

"The next thing we must do is to pack the bubble up," Ashley continued. "I'll just squeeze it until it's really small.

Then we'll put it in your bag, Stephanie, so we don't lose it."

"Wait a minute!" Kristine yelled. "Don't squeeze it yet. I left my binoculars inside."

Ashley and Stephanie groaned as their friend squeezed herself back into the bubble.

"Whew," Kristine gasped as she got back out, clutching the binoculars, "I'm glad nothing happened to them. You never know when we may need another pair of eyes!"

"P-l-e-a-s-e!" Stephanie growled at her. "Forget the smart comments."

Ashley began to made the bubble smaller, just as she had the first time, in her garden. When it was as small as an orange, she handed it to Stephanie.

"Put it in your bag," she said. "But be very careful with it. We need it to get back home."

They were just about to walk out from the bushes when a boy and a girl appeared in front of them. The boy was dressed in shorts and a tee shirt, and he was wearing a Toronto Blue Jays baseball cap. He looked to be about twelve years old. The girl was wearing a dress. She was younger, probably about ten years old.

The boy and girl stared at the three friends. The three friends stared at the boy and girl. No one spoke.

The boy surprised them. He gave a little bow and said, "*Ya.*" The girl also gave a little bow. "*Konnichiwa* ," she said in a soft voice.

Ashley, Kristine and Stephanie were startled. They had never seen anyone bow before, except in the movies. No one had ever bowed to them.

"That's Japanese," Stephanie whispered. "They are saying hello in Japanese. They are being very polite." She spoke to the boy and girl. "Hi, I'm sorry, but we can't speak any Japanese." Ashley and Kristine also greeted the boy and girl.

The boy was smiling now. "Welcome," he said in English. " My sister and I are pleased to meet you. I am Toshio Nishimura, and this is my sister, Kimiko Nishimura."

"Oh, you speak English so well," Ashley exclaimed. "Thank goodness! Well, I am Ashley. These are my friends --- Stephanie and Kristine."

"We learn English in school," Toshio said. "I like to speak English. But where did you come from? You appeared here very suddenly." After a pause, he added, "I know --- you're American, aren't you? Americans --- I didn't think I'd ever meet Americans! That's great!" He was very pleased.

"No, no," said Ashley, "I'm sorry, but you're wrong. We're from Canada. We are Canadians."

Stephanie poked her friend in the ribs. "Don't say he's wrong," she hissed in Ashley's ear. "In Japan it's not polite to say that someone is wrong. Don't be so blunt!"

Ashley blushed. She didn't know what to say next.

Kimiko suddenly looked very happy. "*Hya*!" she cried out. "Oh, Toshio," she said, "we know about Canada. That's where your baseball cap comes from. Also, our father was in Toronto last year, on business. He really liked Canada."

Toshio, too, began to grin. "Do you know Toronto?" he asked.

"Well, we don't live there," Ashley replied, "but we do know it. It's a big city. We live in a small village."

"*Sugoiyo*!" exclaimed Toshio.

"Pardon me," said Kristine. "What was that you said? Su... Sug ... I can't say it, I'm afraid. What does it mean?"

Toshio was very patient. "I said sugoiyo," he replied. "*Su-goi-yo*. See? It's simple to say it. It means 'that's great.' But you can't use that word."

Kristine sniffed. "I can't? Why not?" She did not like being told what she could do.

"In Japan, boys and girls speak differently," Kimiko explained. "A boy can say *sugoiyo*, but a girl must say *sugoiwa*. It means the same. It's just a little different."

"*Sugoiwa*!" Kristine shouted, with a big grin.. "I can speak Japanese! Real Japanese! Listen to me, you guys. *Sugoiwa*! That's great!"

"Kristine, take it easy will you? We don't want you to burst a blood vessel or something." Stephanie thought her friend's behaviour was a bit immature.

"You must meet our parents," Toshio said. "Our father

and mother are just over there. We were flying our kite." He pointed to a field on their left. A huge crowd of men, women and children were busy with kites. "You must bring your parents to meet them," he added. "Where are they? You are surely not alone. Where are your parents?"

"Oh, yes, they're somewhere around," Kristine said quickly. "I just don't see them at the moment ...." Her words trailed off. She wasn't sure what to say next.

"Yes, there they are," Stephanie interrupted. "We are with that bus tour. Our parents are over there." She pointed to the edge of the park. A tour bus was parked there. Some tourists were still on the bus. Others were standing on the sidewalk chatting with the tour guide. The rest had wandered into the park. "They are over there with some new friends," she went on, "but we don't want to bother them right now." She waved in the direction of the tourists. One or two of them waved back. They were probably puzzled that a girl should be waving at them, but they waved back anyway.

Ashley was getting worried. Stephanie had lied. Another lie. When was it going to stop? She did not like to lie. She hoped this Flying Club business wasn't going to get them into big trouble. Only time would tell!

Chapter Eleven

"Come on," Toshio said. "We'll take you to meet our parents." "*Ikou*," he added, with a big smile.

"That means 'let's go'. He's always giving orders," his sister explained. "All Japanese boys are like that!"

"Hm, I understand what you mean," muttered Kristine. "Boys can be like that in Canada too!"

"Oh, Kristine," Ashley said crossly, "why do you say things like that? You're always exaggerating!"

"Well, please excuse my little joke," said Kimiko. "Do come to meet our parents. They will be very happy to meet you."

Mr. Nishimura was a tall man. He was wearing very smart jeans and a white, short-sleeved shirt.

"*Konnichiwa*, children," he said when Toshio introduced them. "Ashley-*san*, Kristine-*san* and Stephanie-*san*, I am pleased to meet you." He bowed to them as he spoke.

"*San*," Toshio explained, "is a word of respect."

Mr. Nishimura turned to his wife. "Michiko," he said,

"these children are from Canada. They have travelled a long way, haven't they?"

Mrs. Nishimura did not speak. She nodded her head and smiled. She was very beautiful, Ashley thought. Her black hair was pinned up and held in place with coloured combs. She was wearing a summer kimono tied with a yellow sash.

"How are you enjoying your visit to Japan?" Mr. Nishimura asked. "There are many things to see. Have your parents taken you to many places?"

"Well ... we haven't had much time yet." Ashley mumbled. "I'm sure we'll see lots."

"Yes, we're sure of that," her friends agreed.

"You must see the Imperial Palace," said Mr. Nishimura. "That is where our emperors have lived for over one hundred years. Look in that direction, just outside the park. That's where it is. It has beautiful gardens and moats."

"A real palace!" Kristine exclaimed. "We've got to see that!"

Mr. Nishimura gave a big smile. "You will enjoy it, but you cannot get inside, of course. But the Imperial Gardens are worth seeing. Also, Tokyo has over two hundred and fifty parks. They are all very beautiful. Most of them used to be private gardens many years ago. They belonged to the emperor's generals. This park is one of them."

Mrs. Nishimura tugged at his sleeve. She whispered something.

"Ah yes," he said, "my wife has just reminded me that there is another famous place you should visit. It is at Kyoto, which is not far from here. It is called the Golden Pavilion. It was built hundreds of years ago as a home for a very famous general. Unfortunately, it was destroyed by fire in 1950. But it has been rebuilt exactly as it was ...."

Kristine didn't hear any more. Mr. Nishimura was a very nice man, but she thought he could be a little boring. She started shuffling her feet.

Mr. Nishimura's story came to an end suddenly. "Toshio-*san*," he snapped, "why are you tugging at me like that? You are shaming me with your lack of manners."

Toshio looked troubled. "I am sorry, *otosan*. ... er, father. I did not mean to make you angry. I thought that our new friends might be hungry ...."

Toshio's words caused Mrs. Nishimura to say a lot of things in Japanese. Her husband turned to the girls when she had finished.

"I am sorry," he said quietly. "Perhaps you have not had your lunch? Please do us the honour of sharing our lunch." He gave some orders in Japanese to Toshio and gave him money. Toshio hurried away. "Toshio will get us some soup," he continued. "My wife has our food. We will picnic over there, in the shade."

Kristine sighed with relief. Her stomach had already

started gurgling. Stephanie didn't care about food at all. She was too busy writing in her notebook. Ashley was so happy that she seemed to be in a trance.

Mrs. Nishimura took food out of a pretty plastic bag that had been on the grass beside their kite. She unwrapped several containers and began laying them on a picnic table.

"Have you eaten Japanese food before?" she asked the girls. They were surprised, because these were the first English words she had spoken.

"No," Kristine replied, "we haven't. We often have Chinese, though."

Stephanie gave her friend a very hard poke in the ribs. Kristine's manners were not good.

"We haven't had Japanese food, Mrs. Nishimura," Ashley said quickly, "but we really want to try it. It looks delicious."

"Let me help you," Mr. Nishimura said. "This is *sushi*. It is cooked rice wrapped in a strip of seaweed. In the middle are tiny pieces of vegetable and fish. Please try some."

Oh, Kristine thought to herself, I'd rather have a hamburger. Stephanie was busily writing the recipe for sushi in her notebook. Ashley took the paper plate that Mrs. Nishimura offered. On the plate, there were two round cakes of rice wrapped in dark-coloured seaweed.

Ashley took a bite. What a surprise! It was truly delicious! She quickly stuffed the rest into her mouth. Kristine and Stephanie were enjoying it, too. "Delicious," murmured Stephanie. "Better than a cheeseburger!" said Kristine, her cheeks bulging.

Mr. Nishimura was delighted. "Excellent, excellent!" he cried. "Ah, and here is Toshio-*san* with the soup."

Toshio was carrying plastic cups which he had bought on the street, just outside the park. He put them on the table.

"It smells so good," Kristine said. "What kind of soup is it?"

"It's called *miso-shiru*, " Mr. Nishimura replied, "but you can say just *miso*. It is soup made from soy bean paste."

For a moment Kristine wasn't sure what to think, but she didn't wait long. She raised her cup and sipped. "Oh, yes! It goes perfectly with the *sushi*. ," she said.

The girls learned a lot about Japanese food. They tasted *yakitori*, which was delicious fried chicken. They chewed happily on *tempura*, which was vegetables fried in a delicious batter. For dessert, they had *manju*. That was a real surprise, because it was cake made out of soy bean. They ate several *manju*!! Only a stern look from Stephanie stopped Ashley and Kristine from eating a lot more!

When they had finished eating, what they needed most of all was a long, long nap --- but, of course, that was not possible! It would be very rude to go to sleep in company! Besides, their adventure was not over yet!

They had arrived safely in Japan, but that was just the

beginning of everything. They were with a very nice family, Ashley thought. The Nishimuras were kind and generous. But how were they going to be able to get away from them?

Ah well, the best thing to do was to relax and to wait and see what would happen. In the meantime, she was sure that she would learn many new things from the Nishimuras.

Chapter Twelve

After lunch, Mr. and Mrs. Nishimura walked over to the pond, where some boys were sailing little boats. The children stayed at the picnic table.

"I'm glad it's the holidays," Toshio sighed. "I get tired of school. Sometimes school seems to be the only thing in my life!"

"Yeah, I know the feeling," Kristine said.

"We rather like our village school," Stephanie remarked. "Is school harder in Japan or something?"

"Pretty hard," he replied. "I have to get up early enough to catch the subway train. In rush hour, the subway is so crowded that guards push the people onto the trains!"

"I've never been on a subway train," Stephanie said sadly.

"We don't have a rush hour in Rosemount," Kristine joked.

"No, and we don't even have bus service either," Ashley added.

"What subjects do you study in school?" Stephanie

wanted to keep on the topic of school. She had decided to write an article on Japanese education when she got back home.

"We study the usual things," Kimiko said. She was tired of letting her brother do all of the talking. "You know --- history, geography, arithmetic, spelling. Things like that."

Toshio gave her a stern look. "What takes the most time is calligraphy," he said.

"Calligraphy?" Kristine asked. "What on earth is that?"

"Calligraphy is writing - hand-writing," Toshio explained. "Writing Japanese is very difficult, because there are special alphabets that are made up of special characters. The characters are more complicated than ordinary letters and must be copied correctly. It's so difficult I have to go to another school after day school - just to learn to write the letters properly."

"Ah, yes," agreed Kimiko. "Juku - that's what it's called. It's a private school our parents have to pay for. I go for music lessons. Almost everybody goes to juku."

"That's not all," Toshio added. "We go to school on Saturdays too!"

When the girls groaned, Toshio said, "School is a serious business. We must stay in school until we have completed high school, and we have many hard examinations to write. We must not fail. If we fail, we bring dishonour to our family."

"Anyway," interrupted Kimiko, "it would be difficult to fail. Our mother is always at the school, talking to the teachers. She finds out very quickly if we do not do our homework, or if we disobey the teacher. Of course, we never disobey the teacher."

Ashley was frowning. "Failure brings disgrace to your family? It makes sense, doesn't it? But I've never thought of it like that before."

"But of course!" retorted Toshio. "Family is important to everyone in Japan. We must honour our parents and make them proud of us. Obedience and hard work are our duty. And that goes for our parents too. I respect my father because he works hard and is loyal to his employer. He leaves the house at eight o'clock every morning and he does not return until ten or eleven o'clock at night. In his work, he shows us that he is an honourable man. We must be honourable in our school work."

He paused for a moment. "It's not all work!" he exclaimed, with a twinkle in his eye. "We have swimming three times a week. Then once a week I get to go to my kendo class."

"Oh, I've seen pictures of kendo, " Stephanie said. "You wear a mask and padding on your body, and you fight with bamboo sticks. I've seen it on television."

"I don't get to do kendo," said Kimiko. "Only boys do that. I have to learn about flower-arranging and setting the table properly. I don't really mind. I don't want to do kendo anyway."

"It's a discipline," Toshio snapped. "Kendo is not just a game, you know. And it's not violent. It's practice in self-discipline!"

Hmm, Ashley thought to herself, boys in Japan can really be so full of themselves at times!!

The conversation was interrupted by Mr. and Mrs. Nishimura, who came hurrying back from the pond.

"Children, children," Mr. Nishimura called out. "Your parents have gone without you! Look, the bus has left!"

Sure enough, the tour bus had gone. There was no sign of the tourists who had been there before lunch.

Ashley came to the rescue. She took a deep breath and told another lie. "It's all right, Mr. Nishimura. We knew that they would go on the bus without us. They left us to play in the park. They were going straight back to the hotel."

"The hotel?" he queried. "Which hotel? Where are you staying?"

This time Stephanie came to the rescue. She had been reading the guide book on Tokyo. "It's the California Inn," she said. "It's just around the corner, over there." She pointed vaguely to her right.

"Ah, that's good." Mr. Nishimura said. "An American hotel. You will be all right, I'm sure. Our hotels look after their visitors very well. Now, come along, and I will take you to your parents."

Chapter Thirteen

Mr. Nishimura drove them to the hotel in his car. Ashley was worried about this. What would happen when they got there? she asked herself. Kristine had a weird expression on her face, and she was rolling her eyes. Not much help there! Stephanie was very quiet.

They had to drive through the Ginza district, which is probably the busiest shopping area in the whole world. The traffic was heavy, of course, because it was rush hour. There were people everywhere. The sidewalks were crammed, and yet everybody seemed to be moving in an orderly fashion. It was amazing that people didn't bump into one another all the time. Mind you, Ashley noticed, the men did seem to push women out of their way rather rudely. She supposed that there were some men without manners everywhere in the world. Her mom wouldn't have let them get away with it, she thought.

"There are over one hundred and twenty-two million people in Japan," Mr. Nishimura laughed. "Some days I think that they must all live in Tokyo!" This was the first real joke they had heard him make.

There were cars everywhere, but there were no problems. The drivers behaved very well. They were patient. They obeyed the signals of the traffic policeman. He wore white gloves and waved at the drivers like a magician. When he signalled them to stop, they stopped. When he signalled them to go, they drove on. He was so entertaining that they could have watched him for hours.

Mr. Nishimura stopped the car outside the California Inn. He turned off the key and started to open the door. "I'll come in and make sure that you are all right," he said.

"Oh, no," Ashley gasped, "we'll be fine. Thank you, thank you."

"Yes, we're okay," Stephanie agreed. "Besides, there's a lot of traffic. We don't want you to get a ticket."

"Gosh, no," Kristine added. "My daddy is so angry when he gets a ticket. His face goes bright red!"

The three girls got out of the car quickly. They said goodbye and ran up the hotel steps. The Nishimuras watched them. Mr. Nishimura had a puzzled look on his face. In the lobby, the girls waited for the Nishimuras to drive away.

"Phew," Stephanie gasped, "that was close." "Too close," agreed Ashley. "And I'm sorry for what we did to Mr. Nishimura. We were quite rude, you know. He expected to meet our parents." "Well, it's turned out pretty well," Kristine observed brightly. "We've had a good lunch.

We've seen Tokyo. And here we are in a posh hotel with brand-new parents!"

"That's not funny," Stephanie snapped. "We've got to get out of here --- fast! It's getting late in the day. We've got to get back to the park."

"The park, the bubble, and home," Ashley said. "That's what I want." She really meant it.

They were about to walk out of the front door when they were stopped by a man dressed in a uniform. He bowed to them and then he spoke. "Young ladies," he said, "excuse me ... but have you lost your parents? Tell me your room number, and I will take you to them."

Oh oh, thought Ashley, here is the punishment for all those lies. I knew it would happen. She couldn't think of anything to say. This time, Kristine saved them.

"Oh, quick, quick," she cried out. "Mom and Dad are just getting on the elevator. Come on ... run and we'll catch them."

The three girls left the startled doorman and raced across the lobby to the elevator. Three or four people were just getting in. When they heard the girls shouting, they held the door open for them.

"Thank you, thank you so much," Kristine panted. "Yes, thank you," said Stephanie. "You don't know how grateful we are," groaned Ashley.

An elderly, white-haired man was looking at them and smiling. "Where are you going in such a hurry, eh?

And where do you want to get off?"

"The next floor, please," Kristine said sweetly. "We are staying on the next floor."

"Here we are, then," the man replied, "home sweet home for you."

The elevator left them in the hotel corridor. No one else was around.

"Life is becoming really difficult," Ashley remarked. "Let's get out of here as soon as possible."

They walked on tiptoe towards the stairs. "We'll just have to sneak back down and get to the park somehow," Stephanie whispered. "We'll be safe on the stairs. Adults never use the stairs!"

The plan did not work. They just reached the top of the stairs when they heard footsteps coming up. Quickly, they turned and ran down the corridor. Behind them, they heard a woman singing a song softly in Japanese.

"In here," hissed Ashley. "Quickly! In here!"

She turned the handle of a door on her right. Luckily, it was not locked. The three friends crept into the room.

But it wasn't a room. There were no windows, and it was pitch black.

"Oh, I don't like this," Kristine whispered in a shaky voice. "Things are getting worse all the time! Where are we?"

"Be quiet," Ashley hissed. "We're in a linen closet. Shh!"

The door was open a little. They watched the maid coming down the corridor. When she reached the closet door, she muttered to herself and banged it shut. Inside, the three girls hid their eyes and held their breath. At last they heard the maid walk away and turn a corner.

"Another close call!" Stephanie said. "If that maid had wanted clean towels or something, she would have found us!"

"Too close for comfort," agreed Ashley.

"For once, I can't think of a thing to say," said Kristine.

"Well, let's wait five minutes," Ashley said, "then we can get out of here."

Suddenly there was a noise like an express train. The whole closet began shaking backwards and forwards. Towels and sheets fell off the shelves all around them.

"Hey," Stephanie called out, "Stop it, will you? I got hit with a bath towel!"

"Watch it!" yelled Kristine in a muffled voice. "Someone threw a bedsheet over me!"

"Ouch!" cried Ashley, "I bumped my head on the shelves."

They were scared to death, but they tried not to scream out loud. They grabbed hold of each other and held on tight. There was danger all around them, and the danger was right there in the closet with them! What was attacking them in the darkness?

Chapter Fourteen

Suddenly the noise stopped. Things stopped shaking. No more towels and sheets fell off the shelves. There was a strange silence everywhere.

The three girls let go of one another. "Oh," whispered Ashley, "what's happened? I don't like this at all." "Same here," added Kristine. "There's nothing funny about this." "It's no good being upset," Stephanie said calmly. "I can tell you now what it's about ......"

She was interrupted by noises outside in the corridor. People were running up and down. They were shouting and calling out.

"Help, someone! Help!" a man shouted in English. "There's been an earthquake! Come and help us!"

"That's what I was going to tell you," Stephanie said to her friends. "The noise and the shaking were caused by an earthquake. Tokyo has lots of earthquakes. Most of them don't do any damage. Actually, that man in the corridor was quite wrong. They're not really earthquakes. They're just tremors ... a bit of noise and shaking, that's all." She tried to sound confident, though she was still shaking from the scare they'd had.

They opened the door of the closet a little bit. There were about a dozen people running down the corridor. They were all tourists, and they were obviously upset. They vanished down the stairs very quickly.

"There doesn't seem to be any damage to the hotel," Ashley remarked. "And those people certainly weren't hurt."

"Yeah? Well, I wouldn't want to go through that again," Kristine grumbled. "Now I really know what it's like to be shaking in my boots!"

"There you go again," Stephanie snapped. "You've always got to make wisecracks. Smarten up, why don't you?"

"Hey, you two, never mind that now." Ashley was speaking very calmly. "This is our perfect chance to get out of here. With all the excitement going on, no one will notice us." Kristine and Stephanie nodded in agreement.

They left the closet and headed for the stairs. When they reached the ground floor, they opened the door to the lobby just a bit and peeked out. There were people all over the place. The hotel guests were upset. Some of the adults were crying. Others were wringing their hands. The children were enjoying the excitement. They couldn't care less about the earthquake. Nobody seemed to be hurt, and there was no damage in the lobby.

"Oh - oh," Stephanie whispered, "there's that doorman again."

He was leading an old lady by the arm and talking to her softly. He took her to an armchair and helped her to sit down.

"He's no problem now," Ashley said. "He's too busy to notice us. Let's go!"

They walked quietly across the lobby. They did not go on tiptoe. They did not try to run. They just walked calmly, as if they were hotel guests. But once they were outside the front door, they ran like the wind!

There were lots of people in the street. There were always lots of people in the street in Tokyo! Now there seemed to be even more. But no one was excited. An earthquake was quite a common thing to them. Certainly, they did not seem to think it was anything to get excited about.

Fortunately, they were not far from the park. They knew where to go, because they had watched carefully when they were in Mr. Nishimura's car. They ran into the park and went straight to the spot where they had landed.

"Okay, Stephanie," said Ashley, "let's have the bubble. I want to go home! NOW!"

Stephanie opened her bag. She had almost forgotten that she was carrying the bubble. She hoped it was all right. After all, they had been through an earthquake --- and lots of other experiences, too ! She gave a sigh of relief when she saw that it was still there and was still in one piece. She picked it out very carefully and gave it to Ashley.

Ashley was a real expert with the bubble. In just a few moments, she had made it big enough for the three of them. They squeezed into it carefully, one by one.

With Pilot Ashley Miller in charge, it was airborne again in the twinkling of an eye. As they floated over the treetops, the sun was just beginning to go down towards the horizon.

"Oh, look," cried Kristine, "the lights! They're beautiful!"

The lights of the city of Tokyo were like a shining carpet below them. There were lights everywhere - coloured neon lights that flashed and danced, bright street lights that shone on crowds of pedestrians, store-window lights that bathed the streets in pretty colours.

"Bye, Tokyo," whispered Stephanie. "Bye, Japan," said Ashley. "Sugoiwa!" shouted Kristine.

Kristine had a very big grin on her face. Hm, she thought to herself, I got the last laugh ... as usual!

Chapter Fifteen

The morning sun was bright and warm. It was perfect weather for flying. The bubble crossed the Pacific Ocean quickly and flew swiftly inland.

Stephanie was sitting cross-legged on the floor of the bubble. She had finished writing in her journal and was now putting on nail polish. Ashley, of course, was flying the bubble. She was smiling to herself as she thought how good it would be to see Brittany again. Kristine was lying flat on her back, with her arms folded behind her head. She, too, was smiling as she whispered *sugoiwa* softly over and over again to herself.

Nobody was talking. They were all too tired to talk. A nice, long sleep would have been welcome, but they were too excited to sleep.

The big excitement was over. The adventure had been very satisfying. Now they were eager to get back home. Of course, with their usual luck, things didn't stay quiet very long. More problems! So what was new?

When they reached the Rocky Mountains, the trip

almost ended in disaster. They got caught in a downdraft again. This one dragged them close to a mountain ledge.

"We're gonna be stranded!" Kristine shrieked. "I just know it. We've had it this time!"

"Kristine! Will you stop that for just one minute," Stephanie yelled. "That's what you always say! Sing a new song, PLEASE! We're tired of the old one."

"Steady on, crew," Ashley murmured in a calm voice. "Don't lose your cool. If we all work together, we'll get out of this fix."

"Well, tell her that!" Stephanie snapped back.

Of course, they were tired. Too much excitement in just a few short hours. That was the problem all right. They were getting on one another's nerves.

Kristine didn't even realise, when she first spoke, what the real danger was. Being dumped onto a mountain ledge was bad enough. None of them fancied scrambling on a ledge of rock like a bunch of mountain goats. But that wasn't the worst of it, by any means. As they hurtled towards the ledge at breakneck speed, an avalanche of snow was crashing down from somewhere higher up the mountain. Tons of snow - a huge river of it, in fact - were heading straight for them, roaring more loudly than any thunderstorm or tornado. Kristine couldn't say a word when she realised just what was happening. Even Stephanie seemed to be paralysed.

The pilot saved them again. With awesome strength,

Ashley managed to steer the bubble out of its fall. Puffing away, with her cheeks as round as balloons, she drove the bubble higher and higher. Very soon, the avalanche was far below them. They slipped cleverly away from the danger.

As you might expect, that wasn't the last bad thing to happen. Next a huge dust storm came at them over the prairies. They had never seen anything like it before.

"Gosh," Stephanie gasped, "it's just like the sandstorms over the Sahara Desert. Can you believe it? I've only seen stuff like this on TV!"

"Oh, look," Ashley cried, "you can't see anything down on the ground. All the topsoil is being blown away."

"It's just like home," joked Kristine, "when Dad does the vacuuming!"

Ashley and Stephanie were not amused. Stephanie didn't like any jokes about the environment. Ashley especially didn't find that joke funny. She was the one who had to steer the bubble high over the swirling dust. That was not an easy thing to do.

When they flew over a beautiful lake, they received the biggest scare of all. They were being shot at!

"Hunters!" Stephanie cried. "Down there, at the lake. They're shooting at the geese."

"Oh, they can't see us," wailed Kristine. "They'll miss the geese and hit us. They'll shoot the bubble down!"

Actually, the hunters weren't really firing very close

to the bubble. It was flying too high to be in real danger. But the noise of the guns was very scary. And the panic among the geese caused a lot of commotion in the sky.

"It's really too bad," Stephanie commented as Ashley steered the bubble out of danger, "that people have to go and hunt geese. What fun can there be in shooting helpless creatures?"

"I know what you mean." Ashley nodded her head seriously. "That's what my dad says too. He says he doesn't see much sport in it."

For once, Kristine didn't crack any silly jokes. She, too, felt bad about the geese.

The three travellers dealt with all of these experiences very well. They were now experienced. They had travelled a long way. They were wise beyond their years. They certainly knew how to deal with emergencies.

But they were very, very glad when, at long last, the bubble glided over Rosemount once more.

"Oh, isn't it lovely," sighed Stephanie. "Everything is so green and so pretty. It's like a picture postcard. It's even better than I remembered. I'm very glad to be back!"

"I just can't wait to get out of this thing," grumbled Kristine. "The first thing I'm going to do is to ask my Dad to cook me a cheeseburger on the barbecue!"

"I can't wait to see Brittany," Ashley said quietly. "I've missed her a lot!"

There was no one in Ashley's garden. She brought

the bubble down softly on the grass near the cherry tree.

Ashley stepped out and threw herself down. She lay with her arms and legs stretched out on the grass. "It's so nice to be home," she murmured, "... so nice to be home."

Stephanie wrote a couple of sentences in her notebook and then closed it with a snap. "It's done," she announced. "My official record of the first flight of the Soapy Suds Flying Club is finished. Now I've just got to put it on the computer."

As soon as Kristine stepped out of the bubble, she started doing cartwheels again ... over by the shed, near the cherry tree, and dangerously close to the flower beds again. Ashley and Stephanie soon put a stop to that!

They were back in their real lives. Once again, time had stood still. Rosemount had not seen them leave, and Rosemount had not seen them return. They had flown over prairies and Rockies. They had crossed the Pacific Ocean. They had visited Japan. But nothing had changed in Rosemount. Everything was just the same. That was the wonderful thing about home. And that was the wonderful thing about having a magic bubble!

Of course, they made the bubble small again, and they carried it carefully back to the shed, where they hid it once more in the old plant pot.

Afterwards, they formed a little circle in the garden, with their arms on each other's shoulders. Then they chanted together: "All for one, and one for all." That marked the official end of their expedition.

"It's all over this time," Ashley declared. "We can go home again. The first great adventure of the Soapy Suds Flying Club has ended."

They had completed the journey successfully, but their adventure affected them all for a very long time afterwards.

As you might expect, Stephanie wrote an article about earthquakes for the school newspaper. Everybody said that it was an excellent article. She seemed to have so much knowledge about earthquakes. They said you would almost think she had been in an earthquake! The article was so good that the editor of the newspaper in the city printed it. It appeared in the weekend edition, which everybody bought because it contained the TV guide. And she got paid quite a lot of money for letting the paper print her article!

Kristine amazed everybody too. She got the recipe for *sushi* from Stephanie and sent it to the women's magazine that her mother read every month. It was a big, glossy magazine, with lots of pictures. The recipe was chosen as the best recipe of the month. Kristine's picture was printed in the magazine. She received a very nice letter from the editor ---- and quite a large cheque! She liked that, because she had never had a cheque before in her life. Her mom took her to the village bank and opened an account just for her.

Ashley won an essay-writing contest because of her trip. She wrote an essay about family life in Japan. That amazed everybody too, because it made you feel as if Ashley really knew what it was like to live in Japan. The essay was so good that Ashley's teacher submitted it to a national essay-writing contest. Ashley won first prize --- and a picture of her receiving a big cheque appeared in the city newspaper!

The big adventure had ended. All three girls became quite well known for their talent. Of course, as Kristine observed, it's a pity they weren't famous enough to be on TV, but that couldn't be helped. After all, as she put it, they could truly say, couldn't they, that travel had been a rewarding experience! For once, Ashley and Stephanie thought that was a pretty funny thing to say.

Of course, this journey was not the end of the Soapy Suds Flying Club. Their adventures were just beginning. They still had the bubble. They could hardly wait for their next flight!

ABOUT THE AUTHOR

The author of this book lives with his wife, who is an artist, on a farm in the Town of Innisfil, Ontario, Canada. They have five horses (named Joey, Lori, Missy, Shira and Storm), a giant Great Dane called Raffi, four house cats - named Archie, Chauncey, Mildred and Nippy - and two barn cats, called Jemima and Vera. It is rumoured also that a family of raccoons live all year in the hayloft of their barn!

The author has six grandchildren. Everybody knows that he could not have written this book without their help!